# Employee Investigations

# by Daniel Barnett

*Published by Employment Law Services Limited, Unit 3, Chequers Farm, Chequers Lane, Watford, Hertfordshire WD25 0LG*

Whilst the publishers and the authors have taken every care in preparing the material included in this work, any statements made as to the legal or other implications of particular transactions are made in good faith purely for general guidance and cannot be regarded as a substitute for professional advice. Any liability is limited to the purchase value of this book or £100, whichever is the greater.
This book achieved #1 status in the Kindle bookstore category for Human Resources, in February 2019

All items produced by Acas are subject to Crown Copyright, reproduced with kind permission of the Controller of Her Majesty's Stationery Office.
Further information about Acas is at www.acas.org.uk.

ISBN 978-0-9553886-3-7

# About the Author

Daniel Barnett is a leading employment law barrister practising from Outer Temple Chambers. With over 20 years' experience defending public and private sector employers against employment claims, he has represented a Royal Family, several international airlines, FTSE-100 companies and various NHS Trusts and local authorities. Employee clients include David & Victoria Beckham's nanny and Paul Mason (subject of the ITV documentary 'Britain's Fattest Man').

Daniel is a past chair of the Employment Lawyers' Association's publishing committee and electronic services working party. He is the author or co-author of eight books, including the Law Society Handbook on Employment Law (currently in its 6th edition). He is the creator of the Employment Law (UK) mailing list, an email alerter bulletin service sending details of breaking news in employment law three times a week to 24,000 recipients.

Legal directories describe him as "extremely knowledgeable and [he] can absorb pages of instructions at lightning speed", "involved in a number of highly contentious matters", "singled out for his work for large blue-chip companies", "combination of in-depth legal knowledge, pragmatism, quick response times and approachability", "inexhaustible", "tenacious", "knowledgeable" and "an excellent advocate".

He is one of the leading speakers and trainers on the employment law and HR circuit. In 2015 he was the keynote speaker at The Lawyer General Counsel Summit in Lisbon and the Pensions & Benefits UK conference in Westminster.

He has presented seminars for the House of Commons, the BBC, Oxford University, HSBC, Barclays Bank, Ocado, and dozens of other organisations in-house.

In 2013, 2014, 2016 and 2019 he designed and was the sole speaker at, the Employment Law MasterClass national tour.

As well as full-time practice as a barrister and speaker, Daniel is an experienced entrepreneur. He is the founder and owner of Employment Law Services Ltd (a legal publishing company), which provides marketing and educational services to employment lawyers and HR professionals. In 2007, he co-founded CPD Webinars Ltd, then the UK's leading webinar training company for lawyers, and sold it to Thomson Reuters in 2011.

Daniel is widely sought after as a commentator in both broadcast and print media on all legal issues, and is the resident lawyer on LBC radio, where he co-presents the legal hour.

**www.danielbarnett.co.uk**
Telephone: 020 7353 6381

'Bad news, I'm afraid. I've been sacked, all bar an investigatory hearing... written notice of a disciplinary hearing, a later appeal and possible tribunal.'

# Acknowledgments

Thanks to Carina Phillips for her help with researching the content and preparing a first draft of this book and the accompanying CD.

I am indebted to Christopher John Payne for his technical advice and assistance.

Finally, a big thank you to Cressie Sugg for proofreading the text, to Jim Chute for his help with design and layout, and to Mike Mosedale for his permission to reproduce his brilliant cartoons.

# Table of Contents

# Introduction

The other day, I saw a mother giving her young son a telling off for hitting his sister. It turned out that the daughter had fabricated the whole thing. The look on that boy's face spoke volumes about injustice; the consequences of not getting the facts right first; of not testing what you've been told. I bet that mother paid out a lot in Haribo that day.

If only a bunch of cola bottles and jelly rings could put right mistakes like that at work. Proper investigations are the cornerstone of good practice when it comes to misconduct, poor performance, and grievances. They are more than a way of an employer keeping out of legal trouble. Good, robust procedures for dealing with problems engender trust among employees. They are more likely to be compliant, to cooperate, and to report problems that might otherwise be ticking bombs in the workplace. Employers who are fair, and who are seen to be fair, win.

An investigation is the classic target for an employee who goes on to build arguments around pre-judgment, corner-cutting, or impartiality.

This book is designed to help those organising or conducting employee disciplinary or grievance investigations. It takes you through the process step by step, covering tricky areas such as the problem of anonymous informers, whether to suspend the employee, note taking and audio recording, how to ask questions during the interview, and concludes with a checklist for writing the investigation report.

If you have any questions or comments, please email me at **employee.investigations@ emplawservices.co.uk**

**Daniel Barnett**
**Outer Temple Chambers, London**
**Reprint, March 2019**

'The next disciplinary committee might not be so lenient.'

# CHAPTER 1

## Starting an investigation

Remember something that not all employers consider straightaway: you don't need to launch an investigation every time an issue presents itself. It's not always necessary. Someone comes to you to report a problem they're having with a colleague. Unless your company policies and procedures require you to take a particular course of formal action, see what informal options may be open to you. Could a quiet word sort the problem out? Could you mediate between two clashing employees? Do you really need to invest in an investigation (it got its name for a reason)?

I'm often asked whether there needs to be an investigation where an employee has been caught red-handed, or where there's really no doubt at all about what has gone on. The answer is that if you want to be safe then, yes, run an investigation on a scale that's appropriate to the issue. The reason is that (a) you need to be 100% sure that you have your facts straight – there's usually a chance, however slight, of things not being quite what they seem. And (b) it gives the employee a chance to offer an explanation and mitigation.

Whether the decision to start an investigation comes from you or from elsewhere, the key is to know from the outset what you're trying to achieve. I don't mean 'let's sack him', although I'm not saying that those words have never been uttered by an exasperated board member. And I don't underestimate HR's job in managing those sorts of expectations, by the way.

As you'll know, an investigation is about finding out the facts that relate to the issue, and determining what did or didn't happen. Key to this is the investigator's job in looking for evidence that supports the allegation and evidence that undermines it (that last bit is important). It's not about deciding what should become of the employee involved – that's for the disciplining officer, if it comes to it. One of your challenges in this is in getting others – not least the investigator him/herself — to understand this. Another is to oversee the process properly while maintaining a safe distance, more about that later.

First step, appoint your investigator. They have to be someone you can trust to do a good, thorough job. They'll need to be logical, careful, intelligent and professional. It might be you. It might be one of your managers. It might be an external consultant. Or even a lawyer (yes, I know: logical, careful, intelligent and professional all at once!).

I've put together a checklist for what you should be looking for in your investigator. They don't need to tick all the boxes, but they should certainly tick a majority.

They should:

- be authorised/required to be appointed under your internal policies/procedures (many policies will require a certain level of seniority)
- be available when you need them
- understand your organisation and how it runs
- ideally have had some investigations training
- be a confident communicator
- not be easily influenced
- not be personally involved in the matter
- not, by their appointment, create a conflict of interest
- not be better deployed at the disciplinary or appeal hearing stage. In a grievance process, however, it often helps if the person who

investigates is the same person that hears the grievance

- be fair and objective
- ideally, but not necessarily, have experience in the particular type of issue you're investigating – eg a compliance officer where the allegation is about a breach of procedure. Having said that, it can sometimes help to have someone who's a bit removed from the subject. It really depends on the type of issue being dealt with.

That narrows it down a bit, doesn't it? Of course, that's in an ideal world. Not all workplaces have an abundance of people who meet these criteria (in addition to people needed at the disciplinary and appeal stage) - small businesses in particular.

Some employers choose to bring in someone to conduct the investigation from outside – usually a lawyer or an independent HR consultant. That's a personal decision, but what I would say is don't spend a fortune appointing externally unless you really have to. Remember that your obligation is to be the reasonable employer. Do what any reasonable employer would do to ensure that the process is fair.

If you're interested in exploring the possibility of appointing an external investigator, I have put together a list of recommended people (all members of my HR Inner Circle and known to me personally) at:

www.members.hrinnercircle.co.uk/
list-of-recommended-investigators

Some people underestimate the importance of briefing the investigating officer. Others shy away from it, fearing they'll be criticised later for being too involved in the process. But I always recommend that the investigator is given really good terms of reference that make the purpose and scope of their role crystal clear. It is also useful to talk through with them some of the dos and don'ts of investigations that I'll cover in this book.

The investigator must understand what is expected of them and, crucially, the limitations on their role and where they fit into the overall process. They cannot, as I said earlier, be expected to follow the 'yep, they did it, now sack them' line, and that might come as a surprise to some. Reining investigators in is a really important part of the terms of reference: and I mean that both in terms of the conclusions they reach and their overall handling of the process from a legal and employee relations perspective.

Showing the investigator an example of an investigation plan can be really helpful.

Acas has a good template that you could use for this:

| | |
|---|---|
| **Investigator** | |
| Terms of reference | |
| **Provisional time-frame** | |
| Policies & Procedures to review & follow | |
| **Issues that need to be explored/clarified** | |
| Sources of evidence to be collected | |
| **Persons to be interviewed (including planned order of interviews)** | |
| Investigation meetings further arrangements (When/where/notes to be taken by) | |
| **Persons to supply own statement** | |
| Investigation meetings to be completed by | |
| **Collection of evidence to have been completed by** | |
| Further considerations | |

Here's an example that I've completed:

| Investigator | • John Smith |
|---|---|
| Terms of reference | To investigate a grievance raised by Andrew A that Annie S has been harassing him in person and by email |
| Provisional time-frame | • Started on 4 June 2015<br>• Report to be completed by 19 June 2015 |
| Policies & Procedures to review & follow | • Anti-bullying policy<br>• Grievance policy<br>• Disciplinary procedure |
| Issues that need to be explored/clarified | • What actions does Andrew consider amount to bullying and why?<br>• What are Annie's responses to the allegations? |
| Sources of evidence to be collected | • Are there any witnessess?<br>• Witness statements<br>• CCTV?<br>• All emails sent between the two which the organisation can still access |

| | |
|---|---|
| **Persons to be interviewed (including planned order of interviews)** | • Andrew A 8 June 9 AM<br>• Annie S 8 June 1 PM<br>• Further names may be added following initial interviews |
| **Investigation meetings further arrangements (When/where/notes to be taken by)** | • Meeting room 1 booked 8th June<br>• HR to be present as note taker<br>• Meeting room 1 provisionally booked for the 11 and 12 June |
| **Persons to supply own statement** | Alison K (internal IT expert): to provide evidence on email interaction between Annie and Andrew |
| **Investigation meetings to be completed by** | 16 June 2015 |
| **Collection of evidence to have been completed by** | 16 June 2015 |
| **Further considerations** | Annie is on paid suspension while the matter is being investigated. |

The investigation plan should set out:

- who the investigator is
- the terms of reference
- a provisional timeframe
- the relevant company policies and procedures that apply
- the issues that need to be dealt with
- the types of evidence that need to be collected
- the people to be interviewed
- arrangements for interview meetings
- the date by when the investigation should be completed
- any other relevant information.

The plan helps focus minds on the job in hand. It will need to be a flexible plan because you can't (and shouldn't try to) predict with precision how things will pan out. So the timetabling needs to be subject to review as the process takes its course. Its use is really in the framework it gives as far as personnel, timings, evidence collection and processes go.

# CHAPTER 2

## HR's Role in the Investigation

C ase law has made it clear that HR shouldn't get too involved because, ultimately, it's the appointed investigating officer's/ disciplining officer's/appeal officer's job to get to the facts and to reach their own conclusions based on those facts.

The reality is that in many organisations the investigator has limited employment law or HR experience. They'll need some hand-holding, but it's important to be careful in how you do that. Help the investigator with the process, but back off on the substance of what they're doing.

We know from recent cases that:

- It is fine for HR to advise on procedure. It is equally fine for HR to advise on the presentation of a report to make sure it's clear and covers everything it should. (*Chhabra v West London Mental Health NHS Trust*).

- It's not acceptable to significantly influence the investigation by suggesting that the investigating officer changes their conclusion of misconduct to gross misconduct. (*Ramphal v Department for Transport*).

- The role of HR should be limited to advising on law and procedure. Anything to do with the employee's culpability should be left to the investigating officer. (*Dronsfield v University of Reading*).

The important point is that a tribunal will need to be satisfied that the investigator was taking an independent, reasoned decision – not doing what they were told to do by HR.

Another important pervasive point is confidentiality, which I'll cover in more detail later on. Don't take it that the people involved in the investigation will instinctively keep the details to themselves. The need for confidentiality should be spelled out in no uncertain terms.

# CHAPTER 3

## How Investigators Approach Investigations

As a manager or HR professional, you'll understand the personalities involved better than many. This means you'll probably foresee problem areas before they're arrived at and will be able to pre-empt problems by gently (or not so gently) guiding your investigator in the right direction.

There are, broadly speaking and generalising spectacularly, three few types of investigators:

- those with a seat-of-their-pants style, who do the bare minimum to scrape by (and who probably decided they were going to say 'guilty' before even reading the documents or interviewing anybody, on the grounds there's no smoke without fire). These types are more rare than they once were, but they're still knocking around.

- the other extreme: those who've watched too many detective dramas, and want to ferret down into every single detail.

- then the dream: the investigator who nails it. These tend to have done it once or twice before – perhaps an important consideration when you're choosing your investigator. But don't assume that experience comes above all else. Experienced investigators can be arrogant and won't take telling what to do. Novices sometimes get it right first time.

These different personalities will handle investigations in different ways, and you need to prepare for this. Whichever type you're dealing with (and bear in mind that you might not have much choice) the investigating officer needs to understand very clearly the extent to which they will be expected to have looked into issues, interviewed staff, and tested evidence.

But what can you tell them? There's no list. There's no matrix that says 'If it's a theft case, you'll need to speak to at least three colleagues, and if the accused says they weren't in work on that day, you must interview their mum'. The overriding consideration is this: it has to be an investigation that is 'reasonable'.

That's all. Just 'reasonable'. But what is 'reasonable'?

We find ourselves defining reasonableness by reference to real-life examples. For instance, would it be reasonable to accept an employee's admission of guilt without question? Sometimes, but not always. Was the confession squeezed out of them by an overbearing manager? (I'm not joking.) Did the employee understand what was going on? Did they know what they were admitting to, and the potential ramifications? A reasonable employer would take reasonable steps to be satisfied that the admission was true and legitimately provided before acting on it and drawing a line under the investigation.

What I can also say is that the more serious the allegation and its potential consequences (eg reputational damage or a criminal conviction), the higher the level of investigation that should take place.

# CHAPTER 4

## Suspension

You have now appointed and briefed your investigator, and I take it that you'll have checked your policies and procedures. But what about the employee? Suspension?

Generally, you can suspend as long as you have good reason. That 'good reason' will normally be one of the following:

- there are health and safety concerns;
- there's a real risk of the employee tampering with evidence or committing further acts of misconduct (credible allegations of dishonesty will usually suffice here);
- working relationships are in a bad shape.

Taking the employee out of the workplace while the investigation is carried out undoubtedly has its benefits. But be prepared to face the employee's argument that 'you suspended me, so you obviously think I did it, and now you're going to sack me'.

There are five ways in which suspension can lead to a constructive dismissal claim or, indeed, a finding of unfairness if you subsequently make a decision to dismiss.

1. If suspension is an inappropriate step, perhaps because there is not sufficient evidence to support the need for it or because the allegation is insufficiently serious.

2. If the suspension goes on for too long, or isn't reviewed at appropriate points. In one case (*Camden and Islington Mental Health and Social Care Trust v Atkinson*) there was a constructive dismissal when the employer did not review the employee's suspension. It ought to have done that, and lifted her suspension, after an allegation against her was no longer in issue. Keep a close eye on whether suspension remains appropriate as time passes. You will be criticised if you keep an employee suspended where that's not reasonable any more.

3. If you communicate the suspension to others in a non-neutral, or inappropriate, way. Several years ago I represented a primary school in a claim brought by a teaching assistant. One of the allegations of constructive dismissal was

that the head teacher, in a letter announcing the teaching assistant's suspension to other staff, mentioned that there were 'safeguarding' concerns – a comment the employee argues was unnecessary and irrevocably damaged her reputation, irrespective of the outcome of the investigation.

4. In very limited circumstances, where keeping an employee on suspension can lead to them losing, or falling behind on, certain key skills. But this is very rare: an example might be an airline pilot who needs to fly a certain number of hours and will lose certification if s/he fails to do so.

5. If you decide to suspend without pay (rather than on full pay) where the employment contract does not expressly permit it. This will always be a breach of trust and confidence. Even if the contract does permit suspension without pay, a tribunal will expect any period of unpaid suspension to be as brief as possible and will scrutinise any delay in the investigation rigorously.

The way in which you communicate the suspension – to the employee and to their colleagues - is key. Make it clear to the employee that it's not a punishment and is just a temporary measure (tell them how long you think the suspension will last) and that it says nothing about the outcome that will be reached after a full and fair investigation. Whether they choose to believe you or not is up to them, but your ongoing actions will need to support the assurances you've given.

Also tell them what is expected of them during the suspension; essentially that they're still employed and subject to employment obligations, but that they are not to report to work and mustn't contact clients or colleagues.

Suspension isn't the only temporary measure you might decide to take while an issue is being investigated. Perhaps the employee's deteriorating relationship with a colleague calls for one or both of them to be temporarily transferred to another department while you carry out the investigation. Watch out for a demotion-type scenario. If the work you ask the employee to do isn't of the same level as they've been used to, you could also be risking a constructive dismissal.

# CHAPTER 5

## Involving the Police

Do you need to involve the police? Few employers want to do this, preferring to keep their problems in-house. But if somebody has been badly hurt in a fight, or has stolen large amounts of money, or there are regulatory requirements requiring the police to be informed, you may have little choice.

More frequently, the police will tell you that they are investigating an incident involving the employee. You have a situation on your hands. Should an employee investigation that relates to the same incident or issue as is being investigated by the police be put on hold while the police do their thing?

I must have been asked this question hundreds of times over the years. The answer is an unsatisfactory: 'it depends'.

There is no hard and fast rule to say that you have to put your investigation on hold when the police become involved. As with so much else, it depends what is reasonable in the circumstances. Internal investigations and criminal investigations are very different processes with very different potential results. The outcome of a criminal investigation might in fact have no impact on the decisions about an employee's conduct, capability or ongoing employability.

But in practice people find it difficult to not link a criminal investigation with an investigation that is happening in the workplace. One of the biggest issues around this is the employee's understandable fear of self-incrimination. If you continue with your investigation and require the employee to give you their version of events, you could find that they are less inclined to cooperate than they might be if they weren't also subject to a criminal investigation relating to the same event. In those sorts of circumstances, it can make sense to hold off on your investigation until the criminal side has been dealt with.

But if you do decide to proceed, the investigator must be mindful of the police investigation and of the potential consequences for the employee.

So what should you consider when deciding whether to proceed or not?

- How important is it that you act quickly? Acas guidance states that "where the matter requires prompt attention, the employer need not await the outcome of the prosecution before taking fair and reasonable action".

- What do your policies and procedures say? There could well be something in there that covers this situation.

- Is it practical to wait? Particularly if you will be paying full salary whilst the employee is suspended, possibly for a relatively extended period of time.

- Could your business cope with the limbo situation of an employee investigation remaining on ice for an unknown amount of time?

Employers need to keep a level head in all of this. Just because the police may be involved, that doesn't necessarily add credibility to the allegations.

Try to treat the two processes – the police investigation and the employee investigation – separately. Even if the criminal case comes to nothing, you may still be justified in continuing with your investigation because, as I said, the question of employability (in a conduct or capability investigation at least) isn't necessarily related to the work the police are doing or have done.

The investigator's focus should be on carrying out an investigation that ticks all the boxes; one that's reasonable, balanced, and that takes into account the seriousness of the issues and the potential consequences for the employee. You can rely on information given to you by the police, but not exclusively so. And in dealing with any third party information, according to the case of *Leach v The Office of Communications*, always:

- decide how reliable it is.

- check the integrity of the person/organisation giving you the information and the safeguards they have in place for ensuring that information is accurate.

- think about the effect of disclosure. How important was it that the information was disclosed to you?

- analyse the information and its implications. Where does it slot into the investigation, and what conclusions might you reasonably draw from it?

# CHAPTER 6

## Confidentiality and Anonymous Informers

Confidentiality has to be at the heart of an employee investigation. It's no good having people involved who can't resist a bit of gossip, or who simply don't think that telling so-and-so will do any harm. And what about those who forget to file their notes away in a locked drawer?

## Protecting Confidentiality for the Employee under Investigation

The investigation must be as confidential as it can possibly be made to be. And that obligation extends to everyone involved, from the investigating officer, to managers, to witnesses, to colleagues who happen to know what's going on. It can be a good idea, particularly where there are concerns about a person's penchant for tittle-tattle, to let those involved know that breaching confidentiality could be grounds for disciplinary action. And enforce that threat if needed.

On one level, maintaining confidentiality shouldn't be problematic because the usual standards of workplace ethics apply. But when it comes to the details of the investigation – for example, the information you give witnesses so that they can answer your questions – it can present one or two challenges. What details can you legitimately withhold so as to respect the privacy of the person under investigation, and maintain the trust and confidence between you? What should or shouldn't you say about what you are investigating?

These are really important points to decide before the investigation gets into full swing. It's not just a respect for privacy issue. It's also to ensure that the evidence you gather is good evidence, and it's not a product of witnesses' behind-the-scenes discussions about the issues. We all know what happens when people talk. What might begin as good, strong evidence can be watered down, or altered completely.

## The Problem of the Witness who Insists on Anonymity

What about the other way round, where it's the witness, rather than the employee under investigation, who might want to have their identity or their evidence treated with a high level of confidentiality?

It depends. Would concealing certain information hinder the employee-under-investigation's ability to represent themselves properly? Would it prejudice the investigation? In other words, would it make the investigation 'unreasonable'?

This can be a difficult call. It really comes down to the details you might be keeping under wraps. I always advise employers to only offer confidentiality as a last resort. That might be in a situation where a witness will only cooperate if you promise them anonymity, because they're afraid of a reprisal or some other negative consequence and they have good grounds for feeling that way. You should never offer confidentiality during your opening approach to potential witnesses.

You will know the characters involved and should have a pretty good idea of whether or not retribution is a real possibility (and if it is, this needs looking into). But remember, too, that your employees have a responsibility towards you. The more senior the employee, the greater the duty on them to report problems and to cooperate.

You may be in a situation where you are forced to give a witness a confidentiality assurance, as that may be the only way of getting their evidence (check the terms of employment first to see if they are under a legal obligation to cooperate in the way you want them to). It's not ideal because it means you withholding certain information from the employee who is under investigation, and that often undermines the basic obligation of fairness and reasonableness. The big question is: if I remove this piece of information, or anonymise a witness statement, will the employee know the case against them and be able to respond to it properly?

Employers are often unsure about whether redacting certain parts of statements will be acceptable to a tribunal. There is a very old, and long established, Employment Appeal Tribunal case called *Linfood Cash & Carry v Thompson* that set out some useful guidance on using anonymous witness evidence. It helps employers tread the line between protecting witnesses ('informants') and ensuring that the person who is the subject of the investigation in a misconduct scenario isn't treated unfairly in the process. Some of the main points to pick out relating to the investigation stage are:

- Put the informant's information – including dates, times, and the detail of what they saw and how they were able to see it - in writing. That will be their statement. Write it out in full; it can be adapted for anonymity purposes before it is shown to anyone else.

- Look into whether or not the witness may have an ulterior motive for giving you the information.

- Do they have a reason to make up or embellish details? Also, what sort of a character are they? Have they got 'form'? Has something happened in the past between the witness and the accused?

- Look for corroborative evidence to verify what you've been told.

- The accused should get to see the anonymous witness statement.

Additional considerations apply if the investigation leads to a disciplinary hearing. The case is worth reading.

Ultimately, the duty of confidentiality is very much a case-by-case issue. It usually makes sense not to give a confidentiality assurance unless you really have to. As I said earlier, don't volunteer it; make it a last resort where the alternative would be that you don't have the witness's evidence at all. Of course, be clear about the value of that evidence. If it's just one more piece of corroboration in addition to the other four statements you've got, don't rely on it. It's not worth the risk of a finding of unfairness.

## The Witness who won't Cooperate

That leads me into another challenging scenario for an investigator: the employee who refuses to go along to an investigation meeting.

If I were to ask you to draw an inference from that, it would be one of these, or maybe all three:

- They've got something to hide.

- They are stalling for time.

- They are just being a pain in the backside.

And you will often be spot on. But they are not the only possibilities. Think about whether there is actually a good reason behind of all that. Are they genuinely worried about speaking out against a colleague? Do they not understand what is expected of them? Are they ill? Is it just that they can't make the time and date that's been proposed?

Offer to rearrange the meeting (especially important where that would be a reasonable adjustment). Take them through the process and how they will be able to help their employer sort the problem out. Ask them to write down their account of what happened in as much detail as possible. These things aren't rocket science, but they do require the investigator to see things from another perspective.

But what if there isn't a good reason for the lack of cooperation? If the investigator is absolutely sure about this then consider grounds for disciplining the employee for failing to obey a reasonable request. Check what the contracts, policies and procedures say about this. And of course, make sure that the meeting request was in fact reasonable.

'Miss Hodges...can you get me the handbook on **grocer misconduct**.'

# CHAPTER 7

## Covert Surveillance

Will it be reasonable – from an unfair dismissal perspective – to rely on evidence obtained by covert surveillance?

It can be, yes, as long as you're not treating the employee unfairly in the process, and it's only done in exceptional circumstances. One big rule here is to be very clear about the evidence you're looking for. Surveillance (or monitoring) in this context should never be used as a 'let's see what we can find' exercise. Make sure that you are justified and sanctioned in what you're doing, with the specific allegation firmly in mind.

And then of course you must use the evidence responsibly, in line not only with rules on data processing, but also in interpreting what it means for the particular employee involved. Let's say, for example, you have an employee who has been off work with a chronic shoulder, but whom you are told has been caught on film playing tennis with moderate gusto. Most employers would assume the employee is taking them for a ride. But that's not a safe assumption to make. The safe thing to do would be to take that evidence and show it to a suitably qualified medical professional. I know, it might sound like overkill – especially where the employee's duplicity could not be more brazen.

In one case (albeit only at tribunal level), *Pacey v Caterpillar Logistics*, the employer had decided that the employee had exaggerated his incapacity. He had been off work with a bad back. Surveillance evidence showed him doing a range of normal things - driving, shopping etc.. He explained that away as his having been advised to do light exercise. That was corroborated by his GP, but the GP wasn't shown the surveillance video.

The tribunal held the dismissal to be unfair. There should have been an occupational health assessment of the surveillance. The employer was also criticised for its handling of the GP evidence. All in all, it was an inadequate investigation that led to an unreasonable conclusion and a bad outcome for the employer. Not what you want! So the lesson is that, in this sort of situation, get an appropriate medical professional to look at the footage and give their opinion on its significance. The courts are unlikely to look favourably on an employer who thinks they know best.

In *City and County of Swansea v Gayle*, the employee had left work illicitly to play squash. He claimed to have been in work at the time. The employer got covert surveillance of him outside the sports centre when he should have been working.

That was a fair dismissal, the Employment Appeal Tribunal held, making some interesting points on the employer's right to privacy:

- the right to privacy is not usually breached by taking photos of people in public places
- an employer is entitled to know what their employees are doing during working hours
- a fraudster can't reasonably expect privacy.

Even though the surveillance in this case wasn't really necessary because the employer had plenty of other evidence of misconduct, that did not negate the reasonableness of the investigation as a whole because it didn't affect the decision to dismiss. Investigations aren't likely to be found to be unreasonable simply for being too thorough, the Employment Appeal Tribunal said.

# CHAPTER 8

## The Investigation Meeting

How should the investigator prepare for the meeting? Or perhaps the question is better put like this: how should you prepare the investigator for the meeting? It is not acceptable for HR to sit back and make assumptions about a person's ability to 'just get' what they're supposed to do. I mentioned in Chapter 1 the investigation plan: that's a great start, and follow it up with a conversation with the investigator to make sure that they understand what they should, shouldn't, must and mustn't do.

Again, Acas has an excellent guide to the interview process which I'd encourage employers to refer to. It shows the steps the interview should take. Essentially:

## Before the meeting takes place:

- plan questions;
- make the logistical arrangements – set a time and place and book a room;
- write to the interviewee to invite them to the meeting and tell them what the position is as far as accompaniment goes (see chapter 9).

## At the start of the meeting, explain:

- who is present, and why;
- the purpose of the meeting;
- the investigator's role;
- the need for confidentiality;
- who will see the interviewee's statement;
- that the statement may be used in the investigation report.

## During the meeting:

- ask questions to get the facts;
- probe, but not in an adversarial way;
- make a note of the interviewee's responses;
- if the interviewee refuses to respond, record that fact, too;
- try to get evidence that may substantiate the information provided.

## At the end of the meeting:

- ask the interviewee if there's anything else they think it's important to mention;

- ask if there are any other people they think ought to be interviewed;

- explain that you might need to follow up with another interview;

- tell the interviewee that they will get a copy of their witness statement to check.

## After the meeting:

- give the interviewee a copy of their statement. Ask them to confirm that it's accurate.

- consider the important facts from the meeting. Is there evidence already collected that supports or contradicts these?

- does any further evidence need to be collected as a result of the meeting?

- do any additional interviews need to be arranged?

# CHAPTER 9
## Things for the Hearing

## Right of accompaniment

There is no statutory right to be accompanied at an investigation meeting, provided there will be a subsequent formal disciplinary or grievance meeting (note that there may be a contractual right to be accompanied, however). But if a formal decision on the disciplinary matter, or the grievance, will be taken at the meeting, then there is a right to be accompanied.

I don't see the point in employers resisting an employee's request to have someone – a family member or friend, even - with them. It can be helpful.

In fact, one case – *Stevens v University of Birmingham* – found that refusing to allow accompaniment breached mutual trust and confidence. But that is unusual. Relevant to the

High Court's decision in that case was that (a) the allegations could have ended the employee's career, so that made it all the more important that he was properly supported; (b) the investigating officer and witnesses had been supported.

## Reasonable adjustments

The duty to make reasonable adjustments applies. That would extend to being amenable to a disabled employee's request to be accompanied, or to allow frequent breaks, to hold the meeting elsewhere, or even to conduct the meeting entirely in writing.

## Note-taking and Audio Recording

I always advise having a word in advance with the investigator about the art and the science of good note-taking (although it might help to have another person present to take notes). Spell out to them the dangers of doodles and stray scribbles. And emphasise the importance that procedural notes play in establishing and justifying a fair process. Witnesses may sign the notes at the end to confirm their accuracy – it acts as their witness statement – so there can't be anything in there that shouldn't be. And there can't be anything missing from the notes that really should be there. The notes have to be a fair and accurate account.

The alternative is audio-recording the meeting. I am a big fan of recording the meeting. HR Professionals tend to dislike it, though, especially if the employee asks for the meeting to be recorded. Whilst all sorts of reasons are given for refusing permission to audio record, the truth is normally very simple: deniability. The person running the meeting wants to make sure the notes reflect that which they want to have occurred at the meeting, and want the opportunity to finesse the notes to make sure they say what they should say.

The problem is: tribunal judges know this, and it can be difficult to explain away a refusal to grant permission to record a meeting if being cross-examined. As for the fear that a recording might be 'doctored', I have never, in over 20 years, experienced a case of an audio recording being doctored, whereas allegations that notes have been doctored are the daily bread of tribunal proceedings. If you're that anxious about an employee doctoring a recording, just make your own simultaneous recording.

## An audio recording has two benefits:

- they are an indisputably accurate record of the proceedings. You don't have the problem of the employee challenging the accuracy of the notes when you send them a copy or, worse, months later at a tribunal hearing

- if you allow an overt audio recording, you won't face the problem of the employee making a covert audio recording. One of my worst tribunal defeats was where an employee pulled his iPhone out his pocket during cross-examination and asked me if I'd like to hear his recording of a disciplinary hearing, where the recording completely undermined the credibility of my witnesses.

Even as little as five or ten years ago, tribunals were cautious about audio recording; they thought it was unusual and not the 'done thing' to record investigative meetings as a matter of course. But nowadays, it is completely normal and accepted as a routine part of any investigation process.

## Evidence Gathering

A witness statement is just one type of evidence. It is also important to collect other sorts, particularly electronic evidence, before it becomes lost, is tampered with, or otherwise becomes less reliable.

Being prepared to act quite quickly and methodically is essential in investigations. An investigator who is comfortable in their role and confident in what they need to do will add huge value here. That said, no one wants an investigator who is gung-ho. Do they know what they can and can't do as far as the monitoring of communications and the handling of data is concerned, including reading employees' emails (avoid the personal ones – that's the key)? I would flag this as a hotspot in the procedure.

## Searching an employee

Only do this in exceptional situations. There must be a clear, legitimate justification to search, and you'll need the employee's specific consent for this to happen (even if you have a contractual right to do it). A refusal to consent could be unreasonable behaviour, but check the reasons very carefully. Keep good notes of all of this.

It is good practice for the employee to be present when you search their desk or cupboard. At the very least, give them that opportunity. If they can't or won't be there, a manager should witness the search.

If there is a criminal angle, you might want to consider involving the police in the search because of their more extensive search powers.

As far as using CCTV or personal employee data goes, check your contracts and policies. If there's no specific right to use this evidence, hold off unless it's not reasonably practicable to establish the facts through other types of evidence. Cost is a factor in reasonableness here.

'I was just giving her a few examples and she passed out.'

# CHAPTER 10

## Questioning During the Hearing

Some of the biggest pitfalls are around questioning. Nobody should expect too much of an investigator who is often just an ordinary employee who has been brought in to do something outside their comfort zone. I recommend giving them a lesson in how to ask the questions that will get the most out of the investigation meeting. Do this generically. Make up a scenario, if you like. Something that will show very clearly the techniques that the investigator could use to get the information they need, in the right way.

Acas has some useful guidance on the types of questions that could be used. I recommend incorporating some of these in your brief. It should help the investigator understand that they are not expected to cross-examine the employee or the witnesses. It is not a grilling. It remains a fact-finding exercise: inquisitorial, not adversarial. So questions that are interrogative (eg 'why did you do that?'), leading (eg 'do you think he was out of control?'), or grouped together (eg 'When you got to work, did you see X straightaway, where were they and what were they doing?) should be avoided.

Here's what Acas recommends:

**Open questions** – Good ice-breakers.

Examples:

- tell me what you heard/saw.
- describe exactly what happened.

**Closed questions** – To get answers to specific questions. Particularly useful if you've got an over-enthusiastic interviewee.

Examples:

- what did X say to the customer?
- where were you when that happened?
- who else overheard?

**Probing questions** – To test the evidence. Avoid aggressive questioning; it's not a cheesy TV courtroom drama, and there won't be any cheers and whoops when the interviewee is finally conquered by a killer question.

Examples:

- you said that you saw X looking shifty. What exactly were they doing?

- tell me more about the way he was loading the pallets onto the forklift.

**Questions about feelings** – These aren't always necessary. Ultimately, it's not about the way this witness felt when a particular thing happened; you're trying to get to the facts. But the answers can add context and help explain the impact of what went on.

Examples:

- what concerned you about X's behaviour?

- why did you feel you had to report the incident?

**'What else?' questions** – Making sure that you have all relevant information. They give the interviewee the chance to add to what they've told you. Supplementing these with closed questions should help rein in a talkative interviewee.

Examples:

- do you remember anything else about the way X was that morning?

- is there anything else you think I need to know?

**Summaries** – End the interview with a roundup of what the interviewee has told you. It ensures that you've understood it properly and it's an opportunity for them to correct anything that may be wrong.

Examples:

- am I right in saying that you saw X going into the accounts office at 3.30pm that day while no one else was in there?
- have I understood this correctly? You drove from head office to a meeting in Yeovil on 23rd June and couldn't have been seen using your mobile while driving because it was in your boot for the entire journey?

It is no good rattling off a pre-prepared list of questions without listening to the answers you're given. Start with a list, definitely, but concentrate on what you're being told. That's a key message for all investigators. It will inform your subsequent questions. It will also mean that you can pick up on points that the interviewee has dodged.

The art of silent listening can be very useful. Few of us are comfortable sitting with one another in silence. If the interviewer doesn't talk, perhaps the interviewee will. It is one way of getting a little bit more out of them. Don't make it weird, though.

Communication is not just about speech, or silence. It is also about the way we act – our body language.

Acas recommends:

- facing the interviewee in a relaxed body posture
- calmness
- not folding arms
- appropriate eye contact
- affirmative facial expressions and gestures (eg nodding).

This is all good advice. So much can, rightly or wrongly, be read into a person's demeanour. I actually spend quite a while advising my clients' witnesses who are about to give evidence at a tribunal hearing about what does and does not go down well – such as the seemingly insignificant (but, oh, so significant) roll of the eyes, the huffs and puffs, and the aggressive stance. It is often involuntary, but needs to be curbed to avoid negative impressions being formed. These things stick, and in an internal investigations scenario, it is fodder for an interviewee's argument later on that there was an element of pre-judgment, or of just going through the motions. It can seem inconsistent with an open mind and an eagerness to give the employee a fair crack of the whip.

This works both ways. Where the interviewee gives off certain signals, these are bound to shape the interviewer's impression of them. But, recognising that body language can sometimes be misleading, the interviewer must be careful to not misinterpret the signs or give too much weight to them. A shifty-looking interviewee, shuffling in their chair and looking anywhere other than straight ahead, is probably nervous, stressed or uncomfortable. The best thing to do in that situation is to ask them if they are ok and try to ascertain the reason (which may well be 'uh-oh, they know I nicked that £50 from petty cash' – I am not saying a shifty-looking employee is never actually shifty).

# CHAPTER 11

## The Investigation Report

An investigation needs to have an outcome.

Once the hard work of interviewing witnesses, gathering evidence, testing people's accounts of what happened, etc. is over with, the investigator still has a job on their hands. With the facts at their fingertips, they must decide what should happen next, within the bounds of their terms of reference.

It is a bit like being a judge in a tribunal case. The conclusion takes time to formulate, and it should require the investigator to pick through the facts with care and precision. They should try and reach a conclusion about what probably happened; the standard of proof is the balance of probabilities, so lower than the criminal 'beyond reasonable doubt'. Is something more likely to have happened than not?

One thing often missing from investigation reports is reasoning: explanations of why the investigator did certain things and reached particular conclusions. This is so useful in showing reasonableness. It sheds light on the investigator's thought process.

If the investigator has been asked to make a recommendation about what should happen next, this should usually be one of the following (and it should never include 'dismissal', 'demotion' or some other sanction; that's for the disciplinary hearing):

- **Formal action**, such as a disciplinary hearing. But formal action could also be about making improvements as a result of issues raised during the disciplinary, grievance or poor performance investigation – for example, a change to a company policy. Formal action could also be carrying out further investigation into something that has arisen during the initial investigation.

- **Informal action**, eg mediation, counselling, training.

- **No further action**.

This will be set out in an **Investigation Report**.

There's no substitute for a really well-compiled, detailed report summing up what was done during the investigation and why - even in the simplest of cases. The investigator should include everything in there, including the reasons that certain conclusions were reached. And remember that the conclusions need to be those of the investigator and the investigator alone.

There's a real skill in writing reports, so do not overestimate your investigator's ability to do this – it's another argument in favour of hiring in an external expert in complex grievances.

> See my list of recommended independent investigators at:
>
> www.members.hrinnercircle.co.uk/list-of-recommended-investigators

Do not assume that even senior staff will know what is expected of them and of the report. Some good practice writing tips from Acas:

- be objective;
- avoid nicknames and jargon and keep language appropriate and simple (sounds obvious but you'd be surprised);
- stick to the facts;

- be concise;
- include all evidence collected;
- explain acronyms. Don't take it that the reader (who, by the way, could be a range of people including the employee under investigation, and perhaps eventually a judge) will know what is meant by these.

Acas has an excellent pro forma that I'd recommend using as the basis of any investigation report. It suggests structuring the report like this:

## Introduction

- Name and job title who authorised the investigation and also of the investigator;
- A brief overview of why an investigation was needed;
- The terms of reference. Include details of amendments made to these.

## The investigation process

- How the investigation was conducted;
- What evidence was collected;
- Could any pieces of evidence not be collected? Why?
- Names and job titles of witnesses;
- Why each witness was relevant?

- Whether there were any witnesses who couldn't be interviewed. Why not?
- Have any witness statements been anonymised? Why? Give details of any enquiries made into that witness's character and background.

## The findings

- Summarise the findings from all relevant documents and from each witness statement.
- What facts have been established?
- What facts haven't been established?

On this point, it is important to distinguish facts that are uncontested from those that are contested. Where they are contested, the investigation report should set out the reasons for preferring one version of events over another.

Where an allegation cannot be substantiated, the consequence of that should be set out: either the investigator cannot draw a conclusion from it, or more investigation is needed.

- Is there any mitigation to consider?
- Any other relevant information to take into account.

## Conclusion

This will depend on the terms of reference. A conclusion might include:

- a recommendation of what should happen next.
- any other recommendations.

Finally, the report should conclude with appendices containing copies of the documents and the witness statements collected and referred to.

## Is that it for the investigator?

Not quite. They might need to discuss their report and its findings with the panel they're reporting to, or with the employee under investigation.

They might also be required to be a witness at any subsequent disciplinary hearing. That role would need to be explained to them very clearly to ensure that they simply present the facts and not their opinion etc.

Employers should capitalise on the expertise an investigator may have acquired along the way. Remember that they are likely to have got to the heart of a workplace issue and may be able to offer valuable insight into how to avoid it happening again, or how to deal with it if it does happen. It is unwise not to take advantage of that. I would always recommend looking carefully at how the investigator may be able to help you adapt your policies and procedures, or suggest training, or some other workplace initiative that might lower the risk of you having to carry out a similar sort of investigation again – because these take time, and they're a distraction.

'Where's the fun in being an employer if you can't spontaneously sack someone anymore.'

# APPENDIX

## Acas Code of Practice on Disciplinary and Grievance Issues

1.  This Code is designed to help employers, employees and their representatives deal with disciplinary and grievance situations in the workplace.

    - Disciplinary situations include misconduct and/or poor performance. If employers have a separate capability procedure they may prefer to address performance issues under this procedure. If so, however, the basic principles of fairness set out in this Code should still be followed, albeit that they may need to be adapted.

    - Grievances are concerns, problems or complaints that employees raise with their employers.

The Code does not apply to redundancy dismissals or the non renewal of fixed term contracts on their expiry.

2. Fairness and transparency are promoted by developing and using rules and procedures for handling disciplinary and grievance situations. These should be set down in writing, be specific and clear. Employees and, where appropriate, their representatives should be involved in the development of rules and procedures. It is also important to help employees and managers understand what the rules and procedures are, where they can be found and how they are to be used.

3. There some form of formal action is needed, what action is reasonable or justified will depend on all the circumstances of the particular case. Employment tribunals will take the size and resources of an employer into account when deciding on relevant cases and it may sometimes not be practicable for all employers to take all of the steps set out in this Code.

4. That said, whenever a disciplinary or grievance process is being followed it is important to deal with issues fairly. There are a number of elements to this:

    • Employers and employees should raise and deal with issues promptly and should not unreasonably delay meetings, decisions or confirmation of those decisions.

• Employers and employees should act consistently.

• Employers should carry out any necessary investigations, to establish the facts of the case.

• Employers should inform employees of the basis of the problem and give them an opportunity to put their case in response before any decisions are made.

• Employers should allow employees to be accompanied at any formal disciplinary or grievance meeting.

• Employers should allow an employee to appeal against any formal decision made.

## Discipline

5.  It is important to carry out necessary investigations of potential disciplinary matters without unreasonable delay to establish the facts of the case. In some cases this will require the holding of an investigatory meeting with the employee before proceeding to any disciplinary hearing. In others, the investigatory stage will be the collation of evidence by the employer for use at any disciplinary hearing.

6.  In misconduct cases, where practicable, different people should carry out the investigation and disciplinary hearing.

7.  If there is an investigatory meeting this should not by itself result in any disciplinary action. Although there is no statutory right for an employee to be accompanied at a formal investigatory meeting, such a right may be allowed under an employer's own procedure.

8.  In cases where a period of suspension with pay is considered necessary, this period should be as brief as possible, should be kept under review and it should be made clear that this suspension is not considered a disciplinary action.

## Inform the employee of the problem

9.  If it is decided that there is a disciplinary case to answer, the employee should be notified of this in writing. This notification should contain sufficient information about the alleged misconduct or poor performance and its possible consequences to enable the employee to prepare to answer the case at a disciplinary meeting. It would normally be appropriate to provide copies of any written evidence, which may include any witness statements, with the notification.

10. The notification should also give details of the time and venue for the disciplinary meeting and advise the employee of their right to be accompanied at the meeting.

## Hold a meeting with the employee to discuss the problem

11. The meeting should be held without unreasonable delay whilst allowing the employee reasonable time to prepare their case.

12. Employers and employees (and their companions) should make every effort to attend the meeting. At the meeting the employer should explain the complaint against the employee and go through the evidence that has been gathered. The employee should be allowed to set out their case and answer any allegations that have been made. The employee should also be given a reasonable opportunity to ask questions, present evidence and call relevant witnesses. They should also be given an opportunity to raise points about any information provided by witnesses. Where an employer or employee intends to call relevant witnesses they should give advance notice that they intend to do this.

## Allow the employee to be accompanied at the meeting

13. Workers have a statutory right to be accompanied by a companion where the disciplinary meeting could result in:

    - a formal warning being issued; or

    - the taking of some other disciplinary action; or

    - the confirmation of a warning or some other disciplinary action (appeal hearings).

14. The statutory right is to be accompanied by a fellow worker, a trade union representative, or an official employed by a trade union. A trade union representative who is not an employed official must have been certified by their union as being competent to accompany a worker. Employers must agree to a worker's request to be accompanied by any companion from one of these categories. Workers may also alter their choice of companion if they wish. As a matter of good practice, in making their choice workers should bear in mind the practicalities of the arrangements. For instance, a worker may choose to be accompanied by a companion who is suitable, willing and available on site rather than someone from a geographically remote location.

15. To exercise the statutory right to be accompanied workers must make a reasonable request. What is reasonable will depend on the circumstances of each individual case. A request to be accompanied does not have to be in writing or within a certain timeframe. However, a worker should provide enough time for the employer to deal with the companion's attendance at the meeting. Workers should also consider how they make their request so that it is clearly understood, for instance by letting the employer know in advance the name of the companion where possible and whether they are a fellow worker or trade union official or representative.

16. If a worker's chosen companion will not be available at the time proposed for the hearing by the employer, the employer must postpone the hearing to a time proposed by the worker provided that the alternative time is both reasonable and not more than five working days after the date originally proposed.

17. The companion should be allowed to address the hearing to put and sum up the worker's case, respond on behalf of the worker to any views expressed at the meeting and confer with the worker during the hearing. The companion does not, however, have the right to answer

questions on the worker's behalf, address the hearing if the worker does not wish it or prevent the employer from explaining their case.

## Decide on appropriate action

18. After the meeting decide whether or not disciplinary or any other action is justified and inform the employee accordingly in writing.

19. Where misconduct is confirmed or the employee is found to be performing unsatisfactorily it is usual to give the employee a written warning. A further act of misconduct or failure to improve performance within a set period would normally result in a final written warning.

20. If an employee's first misconduct or unsatisfactory performance is sufficiently serious, it may be appropriate to move directly to a final written warning. This might occur where the employee's actions have had, or are liable to have, a serious or harmful impact on the organisation.

21. A first or final written warning should set out the nature of the misconduct or poor performance and the change in behaviour or improvement in performance required (with timescale). The employee should be told how long the warning will remain current. The employee

should be informed of the consequences of further misconduct, or failure to improve performance, within the set period following a final warning. For instance that it may result in dismissal or some other contractual penalty, such as demotion or loss of seniority.

22. A decision to dismiss should only be taken by a manager who has the authority to do so. The employee should be informed as soon as possible of the reasons for the dismissal, the date on which the employment contract will end, the appropriate period of notice and their right of appeal.

23. Some acts, termed gross misconduct, are so serious in themselves or have such serious consequences that they may call for dismissal without notice for a first offence. But a fair disciplinary process should always be followed, before dismissing for gross misconduct.

24. Disciplinary rules should give examples of acts which the employer regards as acts of gross misconduct. These may vary according to the nature of the organisation and what it does, but might include things such as theft or fraud, physical violence, gross negligence or serious insubordination.

25. Where an employee is persistently unable or unwilling to attend a disciplinary meeting without good cause the employer should make a decision on the evidence available.

## Provide employees with an opportunity to appeal

26. Where an employee feels that disciplinary action taken against them is wrong or unjust they should appeal against the decision. Appeals should be heard without unreasonable delay and ideally at an agreed time and place. Employees should let employers know the grounds for their appeal in writing.

27. The appeal should be dealt with impartially and wherever possible, by a manager who has not previously been involved in the case.

28. Workers have a statutory right to be accompanied at appeal hearings.

29. Employees should be informed in writing of the results of the appeal hearing as soon as possible.

## Special cases

30. Where disciplinary action is being considered against an employee who is a trade union representative the normal disciplinary procedure should be followed. Depending on

the circumstances, however, it is advisable to discuss the matter at an early stage with an official employed by the union, after obtaining the employee's agreement.

31. If an employee is charged with, or convicted of a criminal offence this is not normally in itself reason for disciplinary action. Consideration needs to be given to what effect the charge or conviction has on the employee's suitability to do the job and their relationship with their employer, work colleagues and customers.

## Grievance

### Let the employer know the nature of the grievance

32. If it is not possible to resolve a grievance informally employees should raise the matter formally and without unreasonable delay with a manager who is not the subject of the grievance. This should be done in writing and should set out the nature of the grievance.

### Hold a meeting with the employee to discuss the grievance

33. Employers should arrange for a formal meeting to be held without unreasonable delay after a grievance is received.

34. Employers, employees and their companions should make every effort to attend the meeting. Employees should be allowed to explain their grievance and how they think it should be resolved. Consideration should be given to adjourning the meeting for any investigation that may be necessary.

## Allow the employee to be accompanied at the meeting

35. Workers have a statutory right to be accompanied by a companion at a grievance meeting which deals with a complaint about a duty owed by the employer to the worker. So this would apply where the complaint is, for example, that the employer is not honouring the worker's contract, or is in breach of legislation.

36. The statutory right is to be accompanied by a fellow worker, a trade union representative, or an official employed by a trade union. A trade union representative who is not an employed official must have been certified by their union as being competent to accompany a worker. Employers must agree to a worker's request to be accompanied by any companion from one of these categories. Workers may also alter their choice of companion if they wish. As a matter of good practice, in making their choice workers should bear in mind the practicalities

of the arrangements. For instance, a worker may choose to be accompanied by a companion who is suitable, willing and available on site rather than someone from a geographically remote location.

37. To exercise the statutory right to be accompanied workers must make a reasonable request. What is reasonable will depend on the circumstances of each individual case. A request to be accompanied does not have to be in writing or within a certain time frame. However, a worker should provide enough time for the employer to deal with the companion's attendance at the meeting. Workers should also consider how they make their request so that it is clearly understood, for instance by letting the employer know in advance the name of the companion where possible and whether they are a fellow worker or trade union official or representative.

38. If a worker's chosen companion will not be available at the time proposed for the hearing by the employer, the employer must postpone the hearing to a time proposed by the worker provided that the alternative time is both reasonable and not more than five working days after the date originally proposed.

39. The companion should be allowed to address the hearing to put and sum up the worker's case, respond on behalf of the worker to any views expressed at the meeting and confer with the worker during the hearing. The companion does not however, have the right to answer questions on the worker's behalf, address the hearing if the worker does not wish it or prevent the employer from explaining their case.

## Decide on appropriate action

40. Following the meeting decide on what action, if any, to take. Decisions should be communicated to the employee, in writing, without unreasonable delay and, where appropriate, should set out what action the employer intends to take to resolve the grievance. The employee should be informed that they can appeal if they are not content with the action taken.

## Allow the employee to take the grievance further if not resolved

41. Where an employee feels that their grievance has not been satisfactorily resolved they should appeal. They should let their employer know the grounds for their appeal without unreasonable delay and in writing.

42. Appeals should be heard without unreasonable delay and at a time and place which should be notified to the employee in advance.

43. The appeal should be dealt with impartially and wherever possible by a manager who has not previously been involved in the case.

44. Workers have a statutory right to be accompanied at any such appeal hearing.

45. The outcome of the appeal should be communicated to the employee in writing without unreasonable delay.

## Overlapping grievance and disciplinary cases

46. Where an employee raises a grievance during a disciplinary process the disciplinary process may be temporarily suspended in order to deal with the grievance. Where the grievance and disciplinary cases are related it may be appropriate to deal with both issues concurrently.

## Collective grievances

47. The provisions of this code do not apply to grievances raised on behalf of two or more employees by a representative of a recognised trade union or other appropriate workplace

representative. These grievances should be handled in accordance with the organisation's collective grievance process.

# HR INNER CIRCLE

# "The HR Inner Circle has improved my life amazingly,

mainly because it means I have to spend less time researching and more time and more time actually doing the work I'm paid for."

**Sue Whittle**, Employment & Safety Advice LTD

## Join to gain access to the monthly HR Inner Circular magazine

jam-packed with amazing information for ambitious HR professionals

# What do you get?

**1** Monthly live online 'Ask Me Anything' sessions: each month, we host an online video webinar, when you can share your HR problems and ask Daniel anything about employment law. You'll also receive a recording and a transcript each month, so you have a permanent record of the session even if you cannot be there.

Please ask your questions now:
1. click 'Raise Hand'; or,
2. type it into the Questions box

> "Daniel Barnett is an inspirational, walking and talking 'how to understand mind-boggling employment law handbook!"

**Ellie King**, HR Manager, RWE Technology

**2** A specially recorded audio seminar every month, with HR shortcuts and workarounds you can't get anywhere else.

**3** The monthly Inner Circular magazine, jam-packed with valuable information for ambitious HR professionals.

**4** Access to Daniel's exclusive, private, invitation-only online Inner Circle group, where you get to discuss HR problems with other smart, ambitious professionals and download precedents and policies they have shared.

"It's the support and help that you get, the reassurance that you're talking to people who know what they're talking about rather than people just randomly giving information."

**Nicky Jolley**, HR2DAY LTD

**5** Access to the exclusive HR Inner Circle website which includes a back-catalogue of all the HRIC resources since the launch in 2015.

**6** After six month's membership, you become entitled to a 30 minute telephone consultation with Daniel Barnett once a year, which you can use for your most urgent and important employment law issues.

**WWW.HRINNERCIRCLE.CO.UK**

"This is one of the best investments in yourself and your career you will ever decide to take."

**100%**
**Risk-Free**
**Guarantee**

Only **£86 + VAT**
per month

No long-term contracts.
No notice periods.
**No fuss.**

*Join today!*

If you are looking for a forum to discuss confidential issues that need prompt employment law advice, then the HR Inner Circle is definitely for you. In addition it offers other tools to help and support. The Facebook group is full of information and solutions to scenarios — invaluable for HR professionals.

- **Sheena Doyle**, Managing Director, The Really Useful HR Company Ltd

It's a forum where you're not afraid to ask stupid questions, even though I'm not usually afraid of doing that. The sheer variety of experience and skillsets ensures there is always an informed discussion. JOIN NOW!!

- **Jon Dews**, HR & Business Partner, Majestic 12 Ltd

If you are looking for a steady stream of thorough, pragmatic, and easily-digestible employment law advice, the HR Inner Circle is a great place to be.

- **Susi O'Brien**, Senior Manager HR, The Action Group

The regular updates are invaluable to not only me, but also my team. We find that they are presented in an easy to digest format and aren't too 'legalistic'.

- **Donna Negus**, Sekoya Specialist Employment Services

There aren't many other employment law advice services where you get direct access to an employment law barrister at a realistic price. Join the HR Inner Circle now – you won't regret it.

- **Kirsten Cluer**, Owner of Cluer HR, HR Consultancy

---

I like being able to use the HR Inner Circle Facebook group to ask other members for a second opinion, or for ideas when I get stuck with solving a tricky situation. There's usually someone who has come across the situation before.

- **Helen Astill**, Managing Director, Cherington HR Ltd

---

When I transitioned from big employers to an SME, I didn't realise how much I would miss having peers to kick ideas around. If you haven't got an internal network, you've got to build an external one. I got so much out of the discussion at an Inner Circle meetup recently and I look forward to getting the Inner Circular.

- **Elizabeth Divver**, Group HR Director, The Big Issue Group

Sign now! The monthly Q & A sessions are invaluable, the magazine is packed full of helpful info, you get lots of goodies and the Facebook page is really informative and a useful sounding board.

- **Caroline Hitchen**, Consultant, Caroline Neal Employment Law

---

Being a member of HR Inner Circle is one of the best sources of HR information and advice, and receiving the monthly audio seminars and magazines is extremely helpful and interesting. I can't recommend becoming a member highly enough. There is a private Facebook group which is great for asking other members advice and sharing knowledge and experiences. I have also recently attended one of the meetups that is organised by Daniel Barnett, and it was good to meet other members (and of course Daniel) in a more social setting. It was also a good opportunity to ask any questions you wanted and being able to get advice or support as to how they would deal with whatever you ask.

- **Tracey Seymour**, HR Manager (Head of Dept), Kumon Europe & Africa Ltd

---

The help and advice from other HR professionals on Facebook is really valuable, and quick. All the team enjoy the audio seminars and magazines for updates on current issues.

- **Catherine Larke**, Director | myHRdept.co.uk

For me it's a no brainer. We have a lot of really good contributors in the HR Inner Circle and it's more than a discussion forum and invaluable source of information. When combined with the magazine, the audio seminars and events, it is a complete service especially with Daniel's legal expertise always on hand.

\- **Elizabeth Ince**, Self employed HR Consultant

Just join! It is invaluable with the resources you have at hand by joining the HR Inner Circle. Especially the Facebook Group where you can get advice or a different point of view that you may not have previously considered, outside of normal working hours which is very useful. Live Q&A's too.

\- **Diana Wilks**, HR Manager, Go South Coast Ltd

HR can be complex because each and every issue will have its own set of individual circumstances. Being in the HR Inner Circle enables you to bounce ideas around and make sure you are considering every angle and aspect, knowing your HR Inner Circle partners will have had a similar experience to share.

\- **Pam Rogerson**, HR Director, ELAS Group

Printed in Great Britain
by Amazon